Fighting Fires

by David Earl

Look at these trucks!
They all help put out fires.

This is a ladder truck.
The ladder can go up,
up, up.

Firefighters
go up the ladder.
They get
as close as they can
to the fire.
Then they use
a hose to spray
water on it.

5

This truck has a pump in it.

The pump pushes water into the hose.
The water can come from two places.
It can come from a tank in the truck.

Or it can come from a fire hydrant.

This truck has a big tank
on it.
Firefighters fill the tank
with water.
They get the water from ponds
or swimming pools.

Fire trucks can get
to house fires.
But if a boat is on fire,
firefighters need a fireboat!

A fireboat never
runs out of water!

Firefighters put out
most fires with water.
But they can put out
fires with foam, too.

12

Foam

This truck can spray foam.
It sprays the foam
if a car or an airplane
is on fire.

This truck can fight wildfires.

14

Sometimes a truck can not
get to a big fire.
But a plane can drop water
on it.

There are many ways
to put out fires!